SHEKINAH IN OUR MIDST

Derrick A. Reeves
Th.D, D.D., Ph.D.

Contents may not be reproduced in whole or in part in any form without express written consent of the author.

SHEKINAH IN OUR MIDST
COPYRIGHT © 1995
BY DERRICK A. REEVES, TH.D., D.D., Ph.D.

ISBN 13: 978-1540669797
ISBN 10: 1540669793

All rights reserved.
This book was published in the
United States of America

Reeverian Concepts LLC

Dedication

I dedicated this book to a very good friend and fellow laborer in the Gospel, Pastor Maurice Broomfield. He has been a lasting friend throughout the years as well as dedicated Prayer Warrior.

For all the times we have talked and prayed together as well as for all our dynamic services together. I will always appreciate and be grateful to God for the pleasure of knowing my friend and fellow soldier.

With Thanks

I can never say thank you enough to my dear family. I have learned over the years that one of the greatest blessings one can have is a family that loves and respects them. I know that my lovely wife and two beautiful daughters are a blessing from the Lord. I acknowledge my family and my God with pure heart. I give thanks and gratitude for God ever being with me and loving me patiently.

Introduction

When we consider the information that is revealed in scripture concerning our God, we begin to understand how awesome He is and how truly ignorant mankind is concerning this awesomeness. There is none who can truly fathom the great mysteries of the Holiness and Majesty of our Lord. He revealed Himself in times of old as Yehovah Elohiym, The Lord God who is the Self Existing One that is All Powerful. This same Lord came in flesh to reveal the mysteries of the unlimited past of Eternity. Because He loved mankind, the record of His love can be seen in the scriptures.

One such record of the actions of our Lord takes place in the Book of Exodus. This booklet is taken from a sermon entitled *"Shekinah in Our Midst."* The material has been expanded and elaborated upon to reveal the principles and concepts to a much greater degree. The writing of this material is presented that you the reader might grasp and comprehend how vast the mysteries of the Lord are.

What does the *"Shekinah Cloud"* symbolize? Why was it visible at various times in the wanderings of Israel? There is great significance in the appearing of the Shekinah Glory. This could also have great significance to the Church of the Lord. If the Church is to excel and grow, she must observe the hidden messages contained within the types and shadows of the Old Testament, concerning the Glory of God in the midst of Israel.

CONTENTS

CHAPTER 1
Unlimited Mysteries of God's Secret Place
Page 13

CHAPTER 2
I Come in a Thick Cloud
Page 19

CHAPTER 3
Vital Understanding
Page 21

CHAPTER 4
Why God Appears in a Cloud
Page 25

CHAPTER 5
His Essence Revealed to The Beloved
Page 29

CHAPTER 6
Secret Chamber in The Cloud
Page 33

CHAPTER 7
What is Shekinah?
Page 35

Chapter 1

Unlimited Mysteries of God's Secret Place

The mysteries of God's secret place are awesomely unlimited and very profound. In scripture, the secret place of the Lord is reflected as being covered by a cloud.

"And Moses went up into the mount, and a cloud covered the mount.
And the Glory of the Lord abode upon Mount Sinai and the cloud covered it six days and the seventh day He called unto Moses out of the midst of the cloud.
And the sight of the Glory of the Lord was like devouring fire on the top of the mound in the eyes of the children of Israel.
And Moses went into the midst of the cloud and got him up into the mount and Moses was in the mount forty days and forty nights."
(Exodus 24: 15-18)

When the term "secret place" is considered, one refers to a place of God that is not available for all to visit neither is it open for all to see. It is a place of express privacy. In Exodus 19:9, the scriptures reveal the mode in which the Lord arrives to an appointed destination.

"And the Lord said unto Moses, Lo I come unto thee in a thick cloud, that the people may hear when I speak with thee and believe thee forever. And Moses told the words of the people unto the Lord."

It is recorded that the Lord proclaimed, *"I come in a thick cloud."* He indicated to Moses that His arrival is accompanied by a concealing element that shrouds the resting place of God in an unobservable realm. All that was present in the sight of Israel was a thick cloud. When these terms are analyzed closer, one can see the original meaning of the text. The word *come* indicates the following:

Bô' (Bo)

1. Come upon
2. Come with
3. To go in

The Hebrew term *bo* expresses an *activity of traveling and carrying something with one or traveling into an arena of something that has a shrouding effect*. The Lord indicated that He come (bow') with or comes upon or goes into the midst of the presence of Moses with a …

Thick Cloud

These two words, *thick cloud* are translated in their original Hebrew language as *'âb ânân*. The âb ânân is the thick cloud in which the Lord would come. The first term that is observed is the word *ab (awb)*. This Hebrew word contains the meaning of:

1. Dark cloud mass
2. Thicket (as a Refuge)

This word expresses something that is dark and covering. It is a mass that can obstruct the view of any discerner or observer. The writer (Moses) uses an expression for thick that is used expressly for a certain type of cloud. The thickness was in the density of the cloud's construction. It was a dark mass that could envelope everything it would move upon. The term used for the word cloud is *'anan (awnawn')*. This term is a word strictly referring to a *Divine act or activity*. It is rendered by Nodhiates and Strong's as being a *Theophanic cloud mass*. A Theophanic cloud mass was *an expressive manifestation of God's presence.* The term *theophany* is *a manifestation of God to man in a form that exemplifies Him as Master and Lord.*

The awesomeness of the very power of God was displayed when the Mount was completely hidden from view. The sight of such power and might in the presence of Israel was indescribable. Those mysteries that were concealed were infinite in number. Mysteries concerning His being, His power, His abilities to manifest Himself, as well as other hidden mysteries were concealed within the cloud. Unlimited knowledge is always available in the cloud of God of Israel. *Anîy Bow' 'Ab (I come in a dark thicket).* He expresses the fact that He comes in a dark cloudy refuge or fortress. He explains to Moses several factors concerning His coming:

1. In His presence, there is safety.

2. In His presence, there is privacy.

3. In His presence, there is a thickness or vast amount of concealment of knowledge of His secret mysteries.

4. In His presence, there is the total unrestrained living essence of God.

5. To know Him unrestrained, one must get to the secret place in the midst of the cloud.

It is there that the naked power of God's Omnipotent Glory can be seen. With all of this glorious revelation of Himself, He still give much more knowledge concerning His person to the man called Moses. He ultimately expresses the Hebrew phrase that reveals a great deal concerning the glory of His *Being*.

Anîy Bow' 'AB 'Anan

This Hebraic phrase expresses the meaning of a *Covenant Maker*, with all that He possesses and is within coming to make covenant with His total essence and this essence is hidden in a dark thicket fortress of a Theophanic cloud of manifestation. He reveals that His presence is so great that it would cause our consciousness to become dark or overwhelmed. The mind of man cannot begin to comprehend God without God's help. Man cannot hope to fathom even the name of the Lord.

Because of limited perspective, man is filled with limited knowledge. In the cloud of God exists the *Expression of Eternity*. If mankind could only understand what significance God set forth when He said *"I come in a thick cloud,"* they could begin to fathom the fact that at this time God revealed Himself in the strongest theophanic expression possible without unleashing the full expression of His Divine Eternal Essence. Although this expression was greatly diminutive of the full expression of His Divinity, it was enough to completely engulf an entire mountain. He came in all His essence, clothed and hidden in a dark thick divine expression.

Chapter 2

I Come in A Thick Cloud

To understand God one must understand that He initially refers to His being as *I*. The term *I* in the Hebrew language is rendered *Anîy*. This Hebraic term refers to the Yehovist name of the pre-existent perpetual God before the *'Echad Dabar (First Word)*. When the term Anîy is expressed it reveals God as Yah. The term *Yah* expresses the personal pronoun that indicates God referring to Himself.

When God speaks of Himself as *I*, He prepares to reveal His desire or His character. The term "I" also designates identification of personal awareness of self. The term "I" designates the total being and all that is present in the total essence of that being. "I" always is used to reflect what one's *choice* or *will* is as well as one's identification. He spoke saying "*I Come… Anîy Bow.*" He made reference to:

1. I, My total Essence come upon…
2. I come with total essential essence.

This total essential essence was the very living energies of God, that which produces life and creative power. All that God was come. He refers to Himself in covenant. He expresses himself emphatically.

Chapter 3

Vital Understanding

It is vital to understand the term *Anîy Bow*, I come. This term always reveals that *the Lord significantly moves with purpose and objectivity.* When this term is used, it always reveals the fact that God comes packed with all of His "Total Essence." It is a given that the presence of God signifies that He plans on releasing something through His Divine Word. God never appears in the realm of man merely for the sake of a grand appearance. When He does appear, it is for the purpose of releasing His nature and for being who He is. When the nature of a being is considered, the Greek terminology used is the word *Phusis*. *Phusis* reveals one's inner characteristics that determine:

1. Behavior
2. Species
3. Character
4. Essential essence
5. Limitations or boundaries of operation

The significance of the term Anîy Bow' is very far reaching in that it portrays the Lord as a fully committed faithful God. He is totally involved in bringing His children to the knowledge of who He is and who they are in Him. He has spared no cost at procuring for Himself a people. When He releases His nature, He releases the power of "generative creation." He is perpetual generative creative life. When this is considered one must consider the need for understanding of this most pertinent fact. The presence of the Lord will always release living energies that generate power that actually constructs matter, as well as perpetually releases the spark of life. This life is that which produces the agents of life and sustains those ethereal eternal energies that produce bios, anima and nephesh in man.

When generative creative life is present, it will always generate life. In the generating of life, death is revoked and disrupted. When death is revoked, the elements of life can naturally begin to function. Because His life is the basis or the spark of life, which all life is produced by, not only does His essence revoke death, but it purifies and fortifies the life that one possesses. This is the reason Israel was highly blessed. (Deuteronomy 28: 1-14)

One must keep in mind that life, in the teachings and precepts of the Hebrew, was holistic and covered the area of total life. If true life if present one will be prosperous, healthy and full of peace. To those in covenant with God, life became much more than merely living physically. It is vital to know that God comes with complete life and total life giving orderly essence (Genesis 1:1-4; John 1:1-5; Hebrews 1:3) for the purpose of establishing a relationship with mankind.

Chapter 4

Why God Appears in A Cloud

"And the Lord said unto Moses, Lo, I come unto thee in a thick cloud, that the people may hear when I speak with thee and believe thee forever. And Moses told the words of the people unto the Lord."
(Exodus 19:9).

This scripture is very clear as to the reason God came in the dark cloud. There are primary reasons and there are hidden reasons for the cloud of God. Firstly, God is an intimately private God. He does not reveal all of His mysteries to everyone. There are those few that God has chosen to speak to concerning His mysteries and these individuals have been especially prepared to be the recipients of those mysteries. Two such cases were Abraham and Moses.

"And the Lord said, shall I hide from Abraham that thing I do;
Seeing that Abraham shall surely become a great and mighty nation and all the nations of the earth shall be blessed in him.

> *For I know him, that he will command his children and his household after him and they shall keep the way of the Lord, to do justice and judgment that the Lord may bring upon Abraham that which he hath spoken of him."*
>
> (Genesis 18:17-19).

Abraham was in covenant with God and chosen, therefore, the Lord revealed His will to Abraham. In the case of Moses, the scripture reveals the following:

> *And Miriam and Aaron spake against Moses because of the Ethiopian woman whom he had married: for he had married an Ethiopian woman.*
>
> *And they said, "Hath the Lord indeed spoken only by Moses? Hath he not spoken also by us? And the Lord heard it."*
>
> *(Now the man Moses was very meek, above all the men which were upon the face of the earth.)*
>
> *And the Lord indeed spake suddenly unto Moses and unto Aaron and unto Miriam, Come out ye three unto the tabernacle of the congregation. And they three came out.*
>
> *And the Lord came down in the pillar of the cloud and stood in the*

door of the tabernacle and called Aaron and Miriam: and they both came forth.

And He said Hear now my words: If there be a prophet among you, I the Lord will make myself known unto him in a vision and will speak unto him in a dream.

My servant Moses is not so, who is faithful in all mine house.

With him will I speak mouth to mouth, even apparently and not in dark speeches and the similitude of the Lord shall he behold: Wherefore then were ye not afraid to speak against my servant Moses?"

And the anger of the Lord was kindled against them and he departed.

And the cloud departed from off the tabernacle; and behold, Miriam became leprous.

(Numbers 12:1-10)

In both cases, these men had a special relationship with the Lord and were given special favor. The special favor (grace) was given because of their chosen office bestowed upon them by the Lord. The statement He makes... *"Wherefore then were ye not afraid to speak against my servant Moses?"* It is here that the Lord teaches us a very special principle. He reveals that He is very private and does not disclose His mysteries concerning His will, plans or purposes to anyone except those He chooses to. It is not given to all men to know the things of the Lord or to come into His Most Holy Sanctuary. He has reserved those secret things and secret places for those He has chosen to reveal Himself to. Since time began very few have viewed the Hidden Secret Parts of the Lord.

To disrobe is to reveal to one what is hidden and exclusively private. The cloud is that covering wherein the Lord conceals those private intimate portions of His Glory. Man at one point in the Garden of Eden was also clothed in the light of the Lord but sin caused his covering to be dissipated. Now man must cover himself artificially with clothing. The Lord covers that which He considers to be personal and private. He reserves these private intimacies for those that have been prepared and nurtured to please Him. The Dark Cloud keeps unholy eyes from viewing those things that are unlawful to speak or for some to see. Certain truths and privileges are only for the eyes of the holy.

Although He would speak to Israel, they were not privileged to see His similitude. He came also to Israel to allow the people to hear God speak to Moses that the people would believe Moses for all times.

Chapter 5

His Essence Revealed to the Beloved

To approach God was a very crucial activity. To come into His presence was to be sure death if an individual was not properly sanctified or invited of God. It is important to understand this principle.

> *"And the Lord said unto Moses,*
> *"Go unto the people and sanctify them today and tomorrow and let them wash their clothes.*
> *And be ready against the third day: for the third day the Lord will come down in the sight of all the people upon Mt. Sinai."* (Exodus 19:10-11).

To give the ministry of Moses credibility the Lord allowed Israel to hear His conversation with Moses. Israel was also allowed to see the dark shrouding cloud completely conceal the mountain called Sinai. The voice that came forth from the Mount called Sinai shook the entire region so that the people were terrified (Exodus 19:16-19). They were allowed to hear this magnificent voice and see the mountain altogether in a smoke because God had descended upon it in fire. The entire mountain shook greatly. (Exodus 19:18) This was the extent of the entire camp's experience. In front of all the camp of Israel, Moses speaks and God answers him by voice.

I find it extremely interesting that Moses spoke when the voice of the trumpet sounded long, and waxed louder and louder. (Exodus 19:19) The loud trumpet blast ushered in the presence of the Lord. God answers Moses from Heaven and immediately comes down to Sinai and calls Moses up into the cloudy inferno. The Lord knowing the nature of mankind instructs Moses to go down and charge or give the people a strict order not to come near the perimeters of the mountain in order to gaze upon the Lord. Here the spirit of God uses the *Râ'âh*, whereas the King James uses *Gaze*. The term *Râ'âh* translates to mean the following:

1. To see intellectually with an eye that examines facts.

2. To view or to inspect.

3. To understand or perceive.

4. To experience or learn of.

5. To be fully aware.

6. To have a position of trust.

It is apparent that the Lord did not desire for all of Israel to gaze upon His glory. When this is considered one can clearly see that there are six things God was not ready for Israel to do. He knew that their hearts were not prepared to examine those spiritual things concerning His Holy Majesty. To behold Him in glory and despise His dominion and authority is to offend the Lord in a most blasphemous way. Only Moses was permitted to:

1. Intellectually examine

2. Inspect

3. Perceive or understand

4. Learn by experience

5. Become aware

6. Be trusted with the visage of God

Because the Lord had great regard for the meekness of Moses (Numbers 12:3) and apparent affection for the man (Numbers 12:608), He did not mind exposing His Glorious Omnipotent Essence. At this point and time only, Moses was so favored to be drawn into the center of the glorious mysteries of the Lord. The Lord revealed His essence to His beloved; a blessing that very few have entered into in the chronicles of human history. If the Church would fall in love with the Lord and reverence Him as Moses did, how much glory could the Church experience in these latter days?

Because Moses held a special place in the heart of the Lord he was blessed to experience the revealed glory of the Lord.

Chapter 6

Secret Chamber in The Cloud

The Shekinah (Cloud of Glory) was the covering of the Lord to conceal those things that were exclusively private and reserved for those special individuals who could be trusted and who would also love and adore Him. The cloud itself was the shroud to conceal the mysteries or things of the Lord. The cloud itself was not the source or power but that which was in the cloud.

It must be clearly understood that with the presence of the Lord there comes a holy atmosphere. He brings with Himself a space of His realm. He breeches through the fabrics of this plane of existence and with Him comes a place where the atmosphere is bombarded with living energies of God's essence. It is a place where no being, man or angel, can enter without the express Word of the Lord. Only when the Lord calls one to "come" can they enter this place. This place is a secret chamber. It becomes an enclosure that is covered by the midst of the cloud, but within the cloud the "Light of Existence" is shone eternally bright. Deep within the cloud Moses beheld The Theophanic expression of the Lord unclothed, unhidden, unrestrained and glorious. In the chambers of secrecy, God begins to unfold His heart, plans and purposes to the heart of His chosen. He unfolds the wisdom and knowledge of His Kingdom. He teaches and trains the alert hearted servant that is attentive to His holy words.

In the "Secret Chambers" of the Lord, one can receive the life and light of God. Being in His presence, there takes place transference of His vital spirit. The exchange of God's life to His servants causes a transmission of the very power of God to be poured out into their very being. With this power comes the abiding expression of God's power, the anointing. As the spirit of they who are taken to this realm are touched and filled with the power of the Lord they begin to shine with the radiant brilliance of the Lord.

The secret chamber is a place of energizing. A place where transformation of character takes place in the lives of the called. This chamber is a chamber of Trans Genesis, where in the origin of one's being is transformed by a new beginning.

In this chamber hidden in the cloud, Moses was transformed from one glory to another by the very power and glory of the Most High God. None of the tribe of Israel could gaze at the events hidden within the cloud. It was a chamber where the Lord uncovered Himself to Moses revealing Himself as the *ÁNÎY HAVAH,* the great *I AM*.

Chapter 7

What is Shekinah?

The Shekinah Glory can be described as a supernatural Theophanic manifestation of God's presence, and yet it reveals much more. To say that Shekinah is just a cloud minimizes what the Shekinah truly is.

The Shekinah reveals to us the concealed realm of God. It is a type of Holy of Holies wherein only those exclusively invited or sanctioned to be there can enter (Exodus 19:21). As glorious as the Shekinah was it revealed God in "Theophanic manifestation." It was not the full outshining of the "Fullness" of the Eternal Essence of the Lord. Shekinah represented a relationship with God where the believer is hidden and completely covered in the life and power of the Lord. It also symbolizes the very merging of one's will into the will of the Lord.

Moses was completely hidden in Yehovah Elohiym, submerged in Him being bathed by His glory. Shekinah symbolizes relationship with God more than anything else. It is the relationship of the blessed where they are taken into a realm of power and spiritual experience of transformation; it is a situation wherein an individual is taken into a realm of power with his God for the purpose of becoming a tool of the God of Glory.

This Shekinah is in our midst. It is the hidden place reserved for believers who dare trust in God and desire a life of servitude with the Lord. The Hebrew term *Shekinah* is actually taken from another Hebrew term *Shakan* and means:

1. He rested
2. He dwelt

The Shekinah actually symbolized the Divine presence of God or the visible symbol of this glorious cloud that rested upon the mercy seat. The Shekinah was a symbol of God's desire to dwell with man and ultimately dwell in man. This Shekinah indicated that the Lord had found a people He could dwell with in peace. To have Him dwell in their midst in covenant relationship was the greatest privilege a nation could ever hope for. As long as the Shekinah was present Israel would have shade from the desert sun and heat against the cold desert air at night and light to lead them at night (Exodus 13:21-22). Israel could rest as long as they saw the evidence of God's presence. When they saw the cloud, the Shekinah, they knew He who is the Lord of Glory was dwelling with them. The Shekinah contained the secret place, that place where life entered consistently.

Israel, like many people today, did not understand that life was the greatest asset of being with the Lord. The Shekinah symbolized, more importantly, everything that was contained in the life of God. Many people seek for many things from the Lord, not understanding that life, in itself, is the initiator of every other thing in existence. When life comes it produces peace, health, prosperity and everything else. Life is the producer of these things. The Shekinah was the life blood of Israel. His life brought them protection, strength, prosperity, provisions and every component of the Covenant. When Israel received God in their midst, they received every provision God had ever made. He gave them the same chance to have life that was given to Adam in the garden (compare Genesis 2:8-9; Deuteronomy 30:10-20). Not understanding what true life consisted of, Adam chose the knowledge of good and evil (Genesis 3:6-7). Israel chose to partake of the tree of personal liberties and thus went into captivity. I find it very interesting that men would rather choose something over life, and yet it happens continually.

The Shekinah is typical of God's presence in the garden. He came to dwell among Israel to bring them life and yet they would never fully understand this purpose of their God. Even today Jesus reminds us that He came to give us life (John 1:4; 5:40; 10:10).

As long as the cloud of God is present in our midst, we have access to the tree of life. The life of God, in itself, contains every aspect of grace a believer needs. It is a pity that men are still choosing every element of grace except life.

The Shekinah in our midst represents this life and the benefits that come from being a partaker of this life. The Shekinah is the visible expression of God in the midst of His people. Let us desire the presence of God in our midst. Let us seek for Him diligently. In so doing we seek for life and the Lord Himself.

Even So, Lord Jesus Come!

Made in United States
Orlando, FL
24 May 2023